I0018841

TABLE OF CONTENT

1. ChatGPT

Function: AI chatbot for conversations, writing help, coding, learning, brainstorming.
For: Beginners to experts (very easy to use).
Free or Paid: Free (basic) / Paid (ChatGPT Plus $20/month).
Website: chat.openai.com
Download: Mobile app on iOS and Android (search "ChatGPT" on App Store/Play Store).

2. Canva AI (Magic Studio)

Function: Graphic design tool with AI
help (like auto-generating designs, text-
to-image, etc.)
For: Beginners, marketers, content
creators.
Free or Paid: Free (limited features) /
Paid (Canva Pro $12.99/month).
Website: canva.com
Download: Canva app available on iOS,
Android.

3. Copy.ai

Function: AI writing assistant for marketing copies, emails, ads, blogs.
For: Businesses, marketers, writers.
Free or Paid: Free (limited) / Paid plans from $36/month.
Website: copy.ai
Download: No download needed (online tool).

4. Runway ML

Function: AI video editing (remove background, create videos from text, AI effects).
For: Content creators, video editors.
Free or Paid: Free (basic) / Paid starting at $15/month.
Website: runwayml.com
Download: Browser-based (no download).

5. Midjourney

Function: AI image generator (create stunning art from text prompts).
For: Artists, designers, creative people.
Free or Paid: Paid only (starting from $10/month).
Website: midjourney.com
Download: Works through Discord (no standalone app).

6. Grammarly

Function: Grammar and spelling
checker with AI writing suggestions.
For: Students, writers, professionals.
Free or Paid: Free (basic) / Paid
(Premium starts at $12/month).
Website: grammarly.com
Download: Browser extension, Windows
app, iOS/Android app.

7. Pictory.ai

Function: Turn text into short videos automatically.
For: YouTubers, marketers, educators.
Free or Paid: Free trial / Paid plans start at $19/month.
Website: pictory.ai
Download: No download needed (web-based).

8. Jasper AI

Function: AI writing assistant for blogs, marketing, and stories.
For: Bloggers, copywriters, businesses.
Free or Paid: Paid only (starts at $49/month).
Website: jasper.ai
Download: Web-based, no app.

9. Lumen5

Function: AI tool to create videos from blog posts or articles.
For: Marketers, social media managers.
Free or Paid: Free (limited) / Paid (starts at $19/month).
Website: lumen5.com
Download: Web-based.

10. Synthesia.io

Function: Create AI videos with avatars talking your text.
For: Companies, course creators, marketers.
Free or Paid: Paid only (starts at $22/month).
Website: synthesia.io
Download: Web-based only.

11. Durable.co

Function: Instantly creates business websites using AI.
For: Entrepreneurs, small business owners.
Free or Paid: Free trial / Paid plans start at $15/month.
Website: durable.co
Download: Web-based.

12. Descript

Function: Edit audio and video files by editing text.
For: Podcasters, YouTubers, content creators.
Free or Paid: Free (limited) / Paid from $12/month.
Website: descript.com
Download: Windows & Mac app available.

13. Remove.bg

Function: Removes background from images instantly.
For: Designers, ecommerce, anyone needing clean images.
Free or Paid: Free (low-res) / Paid for HD downloads.
Website: remove.bg
Download: Browser-based; desktop app also available.

14. QuillBot

Function: Paraphrasing and
summarizing tool.
For: Students, writers, researchers.
Free or Paid: Free (basic) / Paid (starts
at $9.95/month).
Website: quillbot.com
Download: Browser extension.

15. Notion AI

Function: AI assistant inside Notion to write, brainstorm, organize.
For: Students, teams, writers.
Free or Paid: Free trial / Paid at $8/month.
Website: notion.so
Download: Mobile and Desktop apps available.

16. Leonardo.Ai

Function: AI image generation (similar to Midjourney).
For: Artists, game designers.
Free or Paid: Free credits / Paid plans for more usage.
Website: leonardo.ai
Download: Web-based.

17. Suno.ai

Function: AI music generator (create songs from text prompts).
For: Musicians, content creators.
Free or Paid: Free basic / Paid plans coming soon.
Website: suno.ai
Download: Web-based.

18. Murf.ai

Function: AI text-to-speech with human-like voices.
For: Content creators, businesses, educators.
Free or Paid: Free trial / Paid starting at $19/month.
Website: murf.ai
Download: Web-based.

19. Perplexity AI

Function: AI-powered search engine (gives direct answers with sources).
For: Everyone who needs smart answers fast.
Free or Paid: Free.
Website: perplexity.ai
Download: Mobile apps available.

20. PhotoRoom

Function: AI image editor for product photos (background remover, templates).
For: Ecommerce sellers, social media managers.
Free or Paid: Free (basic) / Paid (starts $9.99/month).
Website: photoroom.com
Download: App for iOS/Android.

21. Tome.app

Function: Create presentations and storytelling decks with AI.
For: Professionals, students, startups.
Free or Paid: Free (limited) / Paid coming soon.
Website: tome.app
Download: Web-based.

22. Runpod.io

Function: Rent cloud GPUs for AI
projects (like training models).
For: Developers, AI researchers.
Free or Paid: Paid (usage-based billing).
Website: runpod.io
Download: Web-based

23. Kaiber.ai

Function: Create animated videos from your images/text.
For: Creators, musicians, marketers.
Free or Paid: Free trial / Paid plans start at $5/month.
Website: kaiber.ai
Download: Web-based.

24. D-ID

Function: Make photos "talk" with AI-generated voices and expressions.
For: Marketers, video creators, app developers.
Free or Paid: Free trial / Paid plans available.
Website: d-id.com
Download: Web-based.

25. HeyGen

Function: AI video generator that creates talking avatars.
For: Businesses, educators, marketers.
Free or Paid: Free trial / Paid plans.
Website: heygen.com
Download: Web-based.

26. Opus Clip

Function: AI that turns long videos into viral short clips.
For: YouTubers, TikTokers, marketers.
Free or Paid: Free trial / Paid plans start at $19/month.
Website: opus.pro
Download: Web-based.

27. Writesonic

Function: AI writer for blog posts, ads, and social media content.
For: Marketers, entrepreneurs, writers.
Free or Paid: Free (limited words) / Paid from $16/month.
Website: writesonic.com
Download: Web-based.

28. DeepL Translator

Function: AI-powered translation tool (more natural than Google Translate).
For: Students, travelers, businesses.
Free or Paid: Free (basic) / Paid plans available.
Website: deepl.com
Download: Desktop app, browser extension.

29. Beautiful.ai

Function: Create stunning presentations automatically with AI.
For: Professionals, students, businesses.
Free or Paid: Free trial / Paid starts at $12/month.
Website: beautiful.ai
Download: Web-based.

30. Kuki Chatbot

Function: AI chatbot for entertainment
and casual conversation.
For: Anyone wanting fun AI chats.
Free or Paid: Free.
Website: kuki.ai
Download: Web-based.

31. ElevenLabs

Function: Hyper-realistic text-to-speech voices.
For: Audiobook creators, game developers, marketers.
Free or Paid: Free trial / Paid starts at $5/month.
Website: elevenlabs.io
Download: Web-based.

32. Supermachine

Function: AI image generator focused on commercial use.
For: Businesses, marketers, designers.
Free or Paid: Paid (starts at $19/month).
Website: supermachine.art
Download: Web-based.

33. AI Dungeon

Function: Interactive AI storytelling
game.
For: Gamers, writers, creative minds.
Free or Paid: Free (basic) / Paid
subscription for extras.
Website: play.aidungeon.io
Download: iOS and Android apps.

34. SurferSEO

Function: SEO content optimization tool with AI support.
For: Bloggers, content writers, SEO experts.
Free or Paid: Paid only (starts at $49/month).
Website: surferseo.com
Download: Web-based.

35. Fireflies.ai

Function: AI meeting assistant (records, transcribes, summarizes meetings).
For: Teams, business professionals.
Free or Paid: Free (basic) / Paid from $10/month.
Website: fireflies.ai
Download: Integrates with Zoom, MS Teams, etc.

36. Looka

Function: AI logo and brand design generator.
For: Startups, small businesses.
Free or Paid: Free to design / Pay to download logos.
Website: looka.com
Download: Web-based.

37. Replika

Function: Personal AI chatbot friend.
For: Anyone wanting emotional AI companionship.
Free or Paid: Free (basic) / Paid features.
Website: replika.ai
Download: iOS and Android apps.

38. Play.ht

Function: AI voice generator for audio
articles, podcasts.
For: Bloggers, podcasters, media
companies.
Free or Paid: Free trial / Paid plans start
at $39/month.
Website: play.ht
Download: Web-based.

39. Fliki.ai

Function: Turn text into videos with AI voices and visuals.
For: Content creators, marketers.
Free or Paid: Free (watermarked) / Paid from $21/month.
Website: fliki.ai
Download: Web-based.

40. Poised

Function: AI-powered communication coach (improves your speaking during calls).
For: Professionals, executives.
Free or Paid: Free trial / Paid subscription.
Website: poised.com
Download: Desktop app.

41. Vidyo.ai

Function: Auto-cut long videos into shorts for TikTok, Instagram, YouTube.
For: Content creators, social media managers.
Free or Paid: Free (limited) / Paid from $19/month.
Website: vidyo.ai
Download: Web-based.

42. Soundraw.io

Function: AI music generator for background music and projects.
For: Creators, video editors, marketers.
Free or Paid: Free trial / Paid at $19.99/month.
Website: soundraw.io
Download: Web-based.

43. Wordtune

Function: AI writing assistant to rewrite and improve sentences.
For: Students, writers, professionals.
Free or Paid: Free (basic) / Paid at $9.99/month.
Website: wordtune.com
Download: Browser extension.

44. Claude (Anthropic)

Function: AI chatbot alternative to ChatGPT.
For: Developers, professionals, general users.
Free or Paid: Free / Paid premium coming soon.
Website: claude.ai
Download: Web-based.

45. Adobe Firefly

Function: AI tools for creative design
(text-to-image, text effects, generative
fill).
For: Designers, photographers.
Free or Paid: Free (beta) / Paid later
with Adobe subscription.
Website: adobe.com/firefly
Download: Web-based (in Adobe
Creative Cloud).

46. PromptBase

Function: Marketplace to buy and sell AI prompts (for ChatGPT, Midjourney, etc.).
For: Prompt engineers, AI users.
Free or Paid: Free to browse / Pay to buy prompts.
Website: promptbase.com
Download: Web-based.

47. Gamma.app

Function: Create beautiful documents, decks, and websites with AI help.
For: Startups, business teams, students.
Free or Paid: Free (basic) / Paid plans.
Website: gamma.app
Download: Web-based.

48. Booth.ai

Function: AI generates product photos
for ecommerce from text prompts.
For: Online sellers, ecommerce brands.
Free or Paid: Free trial / Paid.
Website: booth.ai
Download: Web-based.

49. Imagen by Google

Function: Google's AI image generator (text to realistic images).
For: Researchers, developers (not yet public for everyone).
Free or Paid: Closed beta.
Website: research.google
Download: Not available for public yet.

50. Stockimg.ai

Function: Create logos, book covers, wallpapers, posters using AI.
For: Designers, marketers, publishers.
Free or Paid: Free trial / Paid plans start at $19/month.
Website: stockimg.ai
Download: Web-based.

51. Cleanup.pictures

Function: Instantly erase unwanted objects from photos using AI.
For: Photographers, graphic designers, casual users.
Free or Paid: Free (basic) / Paid for HD export.
Website: cleanup.pictures
Download: Web-based.

52. Beatoven.ai

Function: AI generates royalty-free music tailored to your videos.
For: YouTubers, podcasters, filmmakers.
Free or Paid: Free trial / Paid plans available.
Website: beatoven.ai
Download: Web-based.

53. HeyGen (formerly Movio)

Function: AI avatar video creator —
make videos with virtual humans.
For: Businesses, educators, marketers.
Free or Paid: Free (limited) / Paid plans
start at $24/month.
Website: heygen.com
Download: Web-based.

54. Puzzle Labs

Function: Turns complex information into interactive, simple knowledge bases.
For: Companies, educators.
Free or Paid: Paid plans.
Website: puzzlelabs.ai
Download: Web-based.

55. Mutiny

Function: AI personalizes your website for every visitor.
For: SaaS companies, marketers.
Free or Paid: Paid only (pricing on request).
Website: mutinyhq.com
Download: Web-based.

56. Luma AI

Function: Create photorealistic 3D models from simple phone videos.
For: 3D artists, game developers, product designers.
Free or Paid: Free.
Website: lumalabs.ai
Download: iOS app.

57. Genei

Function: AI tool to summarize
academic papers and research faster.
For: Students, researchers,
professionals.
Free or Paid: Free trial / Paid plans.
Website: genei.io
Download: Web-based.

58. Copyleaks

Function: AI plagiarism and AI content detector.
For: Educators, editors, content managers.
Free or Paid: Free trial / Paid plans.
Website: copyleaks.com
Download: Web-based.

59. Spline

Function: Create 3D designs directly in the browser with AI help.
For: Designers, developers, 3D artists.
Free or Paid: Free (basic) / Paid for teams.
Website: spline.design
Download: Desktop app available too.

60. Copy.ai

Function: Write marketing copies, blogs, emails in seconds with AI.
For: Marketers, small businesses.
Free or Paid: Free (limited) / Paid starts at $36/month.
Website: copy.ai
Download: Web-based.

61. Dream by Wombo

Function: Create AI art just by describing it.
For: Artists, casual creators.
Free or Paid: Free / Paid for premium styles.
Website: dream.ai
Download: iOS and Android apps.

62. Humata.ai

Function: Upload PDFs and ask
questions about them instantly.
For: Students, researchers,
professionals.
Free or Paid: Free (limited) / Paid for
larger usage.
Website: humata.ai
Download: Web-based.

63. Wisecut

Function: Auto-edit videos with AI
(remove silences, subtitles, etc.).
For: YouTubers, content creators.
Free or Paid: Free (basic) / Paid plans.
Website: wisecut.video
Download: Web-based.

64. Boomy

Function: Make music tracks instantly
with AI, even if you can't play an
instrument.
For: Musicians, hobbyists, game
developers.
Free or Paid: Free / Paid for commercial
rights.
Website: boomy.com
Download: Web-based.

65. Stability AI (Stable Diffusion)

Function: Open-source AI model to create images from text prompts.
For: Artists, developers.
Free or Paid: Free (open-source).
Website: stability.ai
Download: Via Hugging Face or install manually.

66. Otter.ai

Function: Real-time meeting transcription and notes.
For: Teams, educators, students.
Free or Paid: Free (limited) / Paid plans.
Website: otter.ai
Download: Mobile and desktop apps.

67. Chatfuel

Function: Build AI-powered chatbots for Facebook Messenger and websites.
For: Businesses, marketers.
Free or Paid: Free (basic) / Paid plans.
Website: chatfuel.com
Download: Web-based.

68. DreamStudio

Function: Official website to use Stable
Diffusion for text-to-image generation.
For: Artists, content creators.
Free or Paid: Paid credits system.
Website: dreamstudio.ai
Download: Web-based.

69. Tabnine

Function: AI coding assistant that completes code intelligently.
For: Programmers, developers.
Free or Paid: Free (basic) / Paid for teams.
Website: tabnine.com
Download: IDE plugins (VS Code, JetBrains, etc).

70. Runway ML

Function: Creative AI platform for video, image, and 3D editing.
For: Artists, filmmakers, designers.
Free or Paid: Free (limited) / Paid from $12/month.
Website: runwayml.com
Download: Web-based.

71. Crayon (formerly DALL-E mini)

Function: Generate funny images from text prompts.
For: Anyone wanting quick AI art.
Free or Paid: Free.
Website: crayon.com
Download: Web-based.

72. Jasper Art

Function: AI art generator by Jasper AI.
For: Marketers, content creators.
Free or Paid: Paid ($20/month extra with Jasper subscription).
Website: jasper.ai/art
Download: Web-based.

73. Pictory.ai

Function: Create videos from scripts or blog posts automatically.
For: Marketers, YouTubers, educators.
Free or Paid: Free trial / Paid plans.
Website: pictory.ai
Download: Web-based.

74. Notion AI

Function: Supercharges Notion with AI writing and summarizing.
For: Students, knowledge workers, teams.
Free or Paid: Paid add-on to Notion subscription.
Website: notion.so
Download: Web-based, apps.

75. Papercup

Function: AI voice dubbing for videos in different languages.
For: Media companies, YouTubers, educators.
Free or Paid: Paid (pricing varies).
Website: papercup.com
Download: Web-based.

76. Murf AI

Function: AI voice generator — create realistic voiceovers easily.
For: Marketers, podcasters, video makers.
Free or Paid: Free trial / Paid plans.
Website: murf.ai
Download: Web-based.

77. Replit Ghostwriter

Function: AI coding assistant inside
Replit — writes and fixes code.
For: Developers, coding beginners.
Free or Paid: Paid add-on.
Website: replit.com/ghostwriter
Download: Web platform (no download).

78. Fliki

Function: Turn blog posts into videos
with AI voiceovers automatically.
For: Bloggers, marketers, YouTubers.
Free or Paid: Free (limited) / Paid plans.
Website: fliki.ai
Download: Web-based.

79. Kaiber AI

Function: AI tool for creating animated videos from images and prompts.
For: Musicians, artists, content creators.
Free or Paid: Paid plans.
Website: kaiber.ai
Download: Web-based.

80. SudoWrite

Function: AI writing assistant focused on creative storytelling and novels.
For: Authors, novelists, creative writers.
Free or Paid: Free trial / Paid plans.
Website: sudowrite.com
Download: Web-based.

81. Descript

Function: Audio/video editor where you edit media by editing text.
For: Podcasters, YouTubers, video editors.
Free or Paid: Free (basic) / Paid plans.
Website: descript.com
Download: Desktop app.

82. Elicit

Function: AI research assistant — finds and summarizes academic papers.
For: Researchers, students, academics.
Free or Paid: Free.
Website: elicit.org
Download: Web-based.

83. GrammarlyGO

Function: AI writing assistant that helps draft, rewrite, and brainstorm text.
For: Writers, students, professionals.
Free or Paid: Free (basic) / Paid plans.
Website: grammarly.com/grammarlygo
Download: Chrome extension, desktop apps.

84. Neural.love

Function: Generate AI art, avatars, and enhance images/videos.
For: Artists, hobbyists.
Free or Paid: Free (limited) / Paid credits.
Website: neural.love
Download: Web-based.

85. Play.ht

Function: Generate realistic AI voices and audio content.
For: Podcasters, content creators, e-learning developers.
Free or Paid: Free trial / Paid plans.
Website: play.ht
Download: Web-based.

86. Veed.io

Function: Easy AI-powered video editing online.
For: Content creators, marketers, educators.
Free or Paid: Free (basic) / Paid plans.
Website: veed.io
Download: Web-based.

87. Soundraw

Function: AI music generator where you customize songs.
For: Video creators, advertisers, developers.
Free or Paid: Paid plans.
Website: soundraw.io
Download: Web-based.

88. Piktochart AI

Function: Instantly turn text into beautiful infographics and presentations.
For: Marketers, students, businesses.
Free or Paid: Free (limited) / Paid plans.
Website: piktochart.com/ai
Download: Web-based.

89. Wonder Dynamics

Function: Add 3D animated characters into live-action scenes automatically.
For: Filmmakers, 3D artists.
Free or Paid: Paid (apply for access).
Website: wonderdynamics.com
Download: Web-based.

90. AIVA

Function: AI composing original music based on your mood and style.
For: Game developers, filmmakers, hobbyists.
Free or Paid: Free (limited) / Paid for full access.
Website: aiva.ai
Download: Web-based.

91. Riffusion

Function: Real-time music generation
through AI spectrograms.
For: Musicians, tech lovers.
Free or Paid: Free (open-source).
Website: riffusion.com
Download: GitHub.

92. Writesonic

Function: Create blog posts, ads, and more with AI.
For: Marketers, freelancers, bloggers.
Free or Paid: Free trial / Paid plans.
Website: writesonic.com
Download: Web-based.

93. Lensa AI

Function: AI selfie enhancer and avatar creator.
For: Social media users, photographers.
Free or Paid: Free download / Paid for avatars.
Website: lensa-ai.com
Download: iOS and Android apps.

94. Kuki Chatbot

Function: Entertaining AI chatbot to talk with.
For: Anyone looking for conversation.
Free or Paid: Free.
Website: kukibot.com
Download: Web-based.

95. Genmo

Function: AI creates animated videos from text prompts.
For: Storytellers, content creators.
Free or Paid: Free (basic) / Paid plans coming.
Website: genmo.ai
Download: Web-based.

96. Simplified

Function: AI tools for writing, designing, and social media scheduling.
For: Marketers, businesses, entrepreneurs.
Free or Paid: Free (limited) / Paid from $18/month.
Website: simplified.com
Download: Web-based.

97. Perplexity AI

Function: AI search engine that cites sources.
For: Researchers, students, anyone who Googles.
Free or Paid: Free.
Website: perplexity.ai
Download: Web-based.

98. Clipdrop

Function: AI tool for photo editing
(remove background, upscale, relight).
For: Designers, e-commerce,
photographers.
Free or Paid: Free (basic) / Paid
features.
Website: clipdrop.co
Download: Desktop and mobile apps.

99. You.com

Function: AI-powered private search
engine.
For: Anyone wanting private, AI-assisted
search.
Free or Paid: Free.
Website: you.com
Download: Web-based, mobile apps.

100. Deep Dream Generator

Function: Turn photos into dream-like AI artworks.
For: Artists, dreamers, hobbyists.
Free or Paid: Free (basic) / Paid options.
Website: deepdreamgenerator.com
Download: Web-based.

101. NightCafe Creator

Make AI-generated artworks for study projects.
Free limited, Paid for credits.
Website: nightcafe.studio

102. Dream by Wombo

AI app that turns your text into art.
Free basic, Paid premium.
Website: dream.ai

103 .PromptHero

Get the best prompts for creative AI tools.
Free.
Website: prompthero.com

104. Magenta Studio

Create music with AI if you study arts/music.
Free.
Website: magenta.tensorflow.org/studio

]

105. Soundraw.io

Generate music based on mood or theme instantly.
Paid.
Website: soundraw.io

106. Boomy

Create and release original music in minutes.
Free limited, Paid upgrades.
Website: boomy.com

107. Interview Warmup (by Google)

Practice common interview questions with AI feedback.
Free.
Website: grow.google/certificates/intervi ew-warmup

108. VMock

Smart career readiness platform that reviews resumes.
Free through many universities, Paid otherwise.
Website: vmock.com

109. Resume.io

AI resume builder and templates.
Free limited, Paid premium.
Website: resume.io